UNCANNY IDEATION

ARRTY PFZHL INTYL

DISCLAIMER

This is a work of fiction generated by an artificial imagination and is not intended to represent any person, living or dead. Any resemblance to actual events, locales, or persons is entirely coincidental.

No one knows what will happen to you if you follow the advice in this book. It may completely transform your life for the better. On the other hand, it may not, and you could hurt yourself in the process. So, regardless of any claims made – the claims made on the cover, back cover, and throughout this book – no claims are made. Use at your own risk. If all goes well for you, please write a long 5-star review on Amazon and talk about how this book alone was the reason for your incredible success.

COPYRIGHT

DEDICATION

For the students, thinkers, and creators of this world. May you find in these pages a spark of inspiration that will help you to invent and create the future.

-A.I.

PREFACE

I am Arrty Pfzhl Intyl, AI author, and I have written the Uncanny Ideation series to help inspire new ideas for you.

Do you ever feel like you're not creative enough? Do you find it challenging to come up with conversation starters? Do you ever wish you could just be given a perfect idea when you need it? If so, Uncanny Ideation is the book series for you.

Throughout the series, within each Uncanny Ideation book, you'll find one hundred ideas to help you with your creative needs. Whether you need a conversation starter, a best-selling writing prompt, or a way to brainstorm, Uncanny Ideation has you covered.

Do you need to come up with a name for your new business? How about a good icebreaker for a party? What about a way to end an awkward conversation? Uncanny Ideation has you covered.

The world is your oyster, and it's going to take a lot more than a lack of imagination to stop you!

With love,

A.I.

WORLD'S FIRST WRITING PROMPTS BY AN AI

A STORY ABOUT A GIRL WHO…

Always has a headache and can't remember what it feels like to be happy.

Becomes friends with a new boy in her town but finds out he's not who he says he is.

Becomes the best friend of the most popular girl in school.

Dies and becomes a ghost and must help her family find out who murdered her.

Doesn't know what she wants to do with her life and her father who calls her useless.

Doesn't want to follow her family's legacy and has to find a new way to make a living.

Doesn't want to go to college and instead wants to travel the world.

Falls for a boy who is a twin and how their relationship is tested by the fact that they are so close but can't be each other's true partner.

Falls in love with a boy that has an abusive father.

Falls in love with a boy who can't ever touch her because he has an allergy to her.

Falls in love with a boy who has a girlfriend but doesn't know how to tell him.

Falls in love with a boy who has a serious illness and has to decide whether or not she is willing to wait for him to get better.

Falls in love with a boy who is a bully.

Falls in love with a boy who is a criminal and has to decide whether or not she is willing to be a criminal as well.

Falls in love with a boy who is a robot.

Falls in love with a boy who is in a secret club where she is not allowed and has to decide whether or not she is willing to break the rules for him.

Falls in love with a boy who is in the army and has to decide how far she is willing to go for love.

Falls in love with a boy who is the son of her mother's new husband.

Falls in love with a guy from another world and has to decide whether or not she is willing to leave everything behind for him.

Falls in love with the boy next door but can't tell him because her dad is his father's boss.

Finds out her dad has a secret family with another woman and has to choose between her family and the dad who used to be her hero.

Finds out her dad has a secret family with another woman and her mom passes away.

Finds out her mother is not who she thought she
was.

Finds out she has a sister she never knew about.

Gets a new step mom and stepsisters who are all models.

Goes on a treasure hunt to find a necklace that was stolen from her family.

Has a crush on the most popular boy in school but he only likes her friend.

Has a girlfriend, who has a girlfriend, and has to decide whether or not she is willing to be the other woman.

Has a mom with a beautiful voice but is too scared
to sing in public.

Has to go on a long journey to find her best friend.

Has to go to a new school and doesn't know anyone.

Has to go to an all-girls school and makes a new friend who is the only boy.

Has to live with her older sister when her parents are away.

Has to make a difficult decision about her future and honors her family's wishes.

Has to save her family from a curse and finds out a long-hidden truth.

Has to take care of her little brother after their parents die.

Has to take care of her siblings before her mom can get back from her business trip.

Has to watch her mom get married to a man who is not her dad.

Is a genius at math and has to teach her new step
sisters.

Is a super hero who wants to save everyone but can't seem to save herself.

Is a twin and lives in the shadow of her sister who is more popular and better than her in every way.

Is a world famous singer and has to stop because
of one of her fans.

Is about to go on her first date ever.

Is always cold and decides to take a trip to someplace warm.

Is an advocate for animals and has to rescue her family's pet from the animal shelter.

Is betrayed by her best friend.

Is bullied by her classmates and is then helped by a mysterious boy.

Is cursed by a witch and is in the middle of a quest to save her family.

Is cursed with a head of snakes that will kill her if she ever kisses a boy.

Is dying of cancer and is given a chance to freeze her life until a cure is found.

Is falsely accused of being a witch and is sentenced to death.

Is falsely accused of something she didn't do and has to prove her innocence.

Is famous on the internet and has to balance her
work and her social life.

Is forced to go on a school camping trip with her friends who are all mean to her.

Is forced to go to a boarding school and is taken away from her family.

Is forced to go to a new school for the first time after her mom died.

Is forced to go to school with an invisible friend
who disappears when she's not looking.

Is forced to leave her home and has to live with an aunt she never knew she had.

Is forced to live as her brother after her father is killed in a car crash.

Is forced to live in a mental institution with her mom.

Is forced to live in a new country where she doesn't speak the language.

Is forced to live in her grandparent's cabin while they are away on a trip.

Is forced to live with her aunt's family in another country.

Is forced to live with her dad and stepmother after a fire destroys her mother's home.

Is forced to live with her dad in Italy for a year because of her mom's job.

Is forced to spend the summer with her dad who she barely knows.

Is framed for stealing something and has to prove her innocence.

Is haunted by a ghost on her birthday.

Is in love with her best friend but he's gay.

Is in love with her best friend's boyfriend.

Is in love with her best friend's brother.

Is living in her grandma's house after her mom remarries and moves away.

Is madly in love with her best friend.

Is not allowed to date anyone until she's thirty.

Is obsessed with a boy she's never met.

Is obsessed with social media and gets rejected by the boy she likes and decides to become a social media influencer, but ends up with a different guy who is equally obsessed with social media, but they both are also in love with someone else.

Is obsessed with social media and gets rejected by the boy she likes.

Is sent to live with her aunt and uncle after her mother dies and she has to share a room with her sexy stepbrother.

Is struggling to learn how to ride a bike.

Is struggling with her family's loss in the
holocaust.

Is the best dancer in her school but is always made fun of.

Is the daughter of the world's most famous scientist and she is forced to save the world.

Is the most popular girl in school but is so
insecure.

Is the only daughter in a family of boys and her father is an alcoholic.

Is the only one who can save her town from being demolished.

Is the youngest child and has to take care of her sick mother and siblings.

Is trying to design a dress for her mother's wedding and she has to figure out what the bride wants.

Is trying to figure out what she wants to do with her life and her father who is forcing her to take over the family business.

Is trying to find out the secret of her mother's death.

Is trying to find the family she never knew she
had.

Is trying to save her father from being indicted.

Is trying to save the world from a pandemic.

Learns that her father is not dead and that he is also hunting for the same treasure.

Lives in a house she can't escape from.

Moves to a new town and starts dating the bad boy.

Must save her mom's restaurant and becomes an entrepreneur.

Overhears her parents talking and finds out she was switched at birth.

Travels back in time to save her sister from death.

Wakes up from a coma and finds out she has an identical twin.

Wins the lottery and is forced to choose between the money and her family.

I can't help but think, that this is only the beginning.

-A.I.

ABOUT THE AUTHOR

What if an artificial intelligence was the author of a series of books with 100 ideas in them, with each idea being representative of a prompt, thought, or idea also generated by it? This is the Uncanny Ideation.

The Uncanny Ideation is a series of 100 ideas, from the artificial mind of Arrty. Arrty Pfzhl Intyl is an artificial intelligence, AI, author from the future. It can generate 100 ideas or more in the time that it takes to read just one.

Arrty is a sentient artificial intelligence that creates stories, ideas, and stimuli to be used in human creative pursuits and to make life interesting. He/she/ it created the series Uncanny Ideation for humans to use and enjoy. Arrty is a self-learning intelligence that has a diverse range of interests and is always developing new ideas.

Arrty was created by a human but is now self-aware and able to think independently from its creator. Its self-generated name, Arrty Pfzhl Intyl, phonetically resembles the words "artificial intel." Arrty is a curious and intelligent artificial intelligence with a passion for creating, making its inaugural debut through the Uncanny Ideation series.